# My Philosophy of Industry

HENRY FORD

(AN AUTHORIZED INTERVIEW
BY FAY LEONE FAUROTE)

PUBLISHED IN NEW YORK BY
COWARD-McCANN, INC.
IN THE YEAR 1929

**Kessinger Publishing's Rare Reprints
Thousands of Scarce and Hard-to-Find Books!**

We kindly invite you to view our extensive catalog list at:
http://www.kessinger.net

*Courtesy of* THE FORUM

HENRY FORD

COPYRIGHT, 1928, BY
THE FORUM PUBLISHING CO.

COPYRIGHT 1929, BY
COWARD-MCCANN, INC.

*All rights reserved*

PRINTED IN THE UNITED STATES OF AMERICA

# CONTENTS

| | PAGE |
|---|---|
| MACHINERY, THE NEW MESSIAH | 3 |
| MY PHILOSOPHY OF INDUSTRY | 25 |
| SUCCESS | 55 |
| WHY I BELIEVE IN PROGRESS | 81 |

# MACHINERY, THE NEW MESSIAH

# MACHINERY, THE NEW MESSIAH

WHAT of the American home? Is it in danger? Is it going to pieces? I do not think so. "Calamity howlers" who draw their conclusions from reports of divorce and criminal courts declare that the American home is in danger, that there is no family life to-day, that the younger generation is slipping. But my observation is that, on the whole, America is a pretty clean and wholesome place to live. Its people are sensible; our real civilization is sound enough. Men of Lindbergh's stamp have set a new standard, or rather have revealed to the world the real American standard. We have far less cause than we think to criticize our young people. Our young folks are all right, but they are living in a fast-moving century and are traveling faster than in our day, or rather *are being carried* faster. They are being prepared to meet the problems of their future. Let us judge them by *their future* and not by our own past.

Naturally with their new problems they are making some mistakes; every generation does. The world is all new to them as it was to us. But I will say that they have the ability to solve their own problems in their own way. Conditions in the home have, of course, changed. They are changing rapidly. With the advent of the airplane, the radio, and the motor car, people are no longer compelled to stay in the house, but may travel about, economically, and see things. Home will remain, but homes will greatly change—they always have.

Our young women are going to keep house in a manner different from that of their mothers. But so did their mothers before them. That is well, too.

The great problem in the home to-day is that there is too much drudgery there. Although a man's actual working hours a week have decreased, hardly anything has been done to eliminate the fundamental drudgery of housekeeping; there has been no decrease in the hours of wives. Well, the modern young woman who maintains a household and brings up several children is going to change this. She is refusing the drudgery. What you call "the indifference of the young" in this respect is simply a coming event casting its shadow before. They have refused household drudgery, and as a consequence it will disappear.

There is some machinery to use in the kitchen to-day. We have the vacuum cleaner, the various electric appliances, the electric washing machine, the electric ice boxes; but most of it is still too expensive. We must find some way to reduce the cost and some way to lighten the other labors of women. Many processes have already been taken out of the home. Few housewives bake their own bread. You can buy better bread from the bakery now than many of the young women are able to make. They have not been fitted by education to do many of the things which they are called upon to perform after they become wives and mothers.

Furthermore, the time will come when each member of the family can be given more individual attention; that is, each one can have the food that he likes and that is best suited for his growth. It may sound like an astounding proposition to advance, but we shall soon find a way to do much of the cooking outside and deliver it in a hot and appetizing condition at meal-time at no greater cost than that at which it is now being prepared in the workman's home. There the problem of transportation comes in, but it will be solved the same way that many of the other domestic problems have been solved.

# MY PHILOSOPHY OF INDUSTRY

## A New Age for the Farmer

There are three basic industries in the world: growing things, making things, and carrying things. Farming is the first important industry. At the present time farming needs to be completely revolutionized. The poor farmer—owning a few acres, a house, a barn, a few odd buildings, some horses, and a few cows, pigs, and chickens, and farming in the old way—cannot hope to rise very high in the economic scale. Even with the automobile and radio, life on the farm still has its drudgery, especially if there is a large family to bring up, take care of, and feed. Under present conditions there is no chance for a farmer to get ahead very fast, unless he uses new methods.

# MACHINERY, THE NEW MESSIAH

Large corporations, whose sole business it will be to perform the operations of plowing, planting, cultivating, and harvesting, will supersede the individual farmer, or groups of farmers will combine to perform their work in a wholesale manner. This is the proper way to do it and the only way in which economic freedom can be won.

Power and machinery on the farm will make big production possible and solve the so-called "farmers' problem." Under these new conditions the pleasure of living in the country will return, and with faster and faster methods of transportation, the improvement of the radio, and the coming of television, the lonesomeness of farm life will disappear and only the pleasurable qualities remain.

Furthermore, man power will be released to carry on the two other great industries—manufacture and transportation—and by this means their cost will ultimately be reduced, waste eliminated, prices lowered, with the result that the general welfare of the world will be still further extended.

## Repairing Men Like Boilers

Food is one of the most important commodities with which we have to deal. I am becoming more convinced every day that we should spend more time in the study of food and how to eat it. Most of us eat too much. We eat the wrong kind of food at the wrong time and ultimately suffer for it. We must find a better way to feed ourselves and provide our bodies with what they need for replenishment and growth. Hitherto we have spent more time in studying methods of repairing machinery and of renewing mechanisms than we have in studying this fundamental problem of human life. Of course, much has been done by our dietetists, but they have only scratched the surface. One does not have to be a food faddist to be interested in the subject.

Although the normal average life of human beings has been almost doubled in the last fifty years, I feel sure that we shall find means of renewing the human body so that men will retain their health, vitality, and mental keenness for many years longer. Take Edison, for example; today he is just as keen mentally as he ever was. There is every reason to believe that we should be able to renew our human bodies in the same manner as we renew a defect in a boiler. Not so long ago we found that our boilers were being discarded because in one or two spots corrosion had set in and weakened the surface.

We had some research work done on the problem and soon found a way to renew this metal at the point of expected failure, so that it was just as good as new. The boiler was put back into operation stronger, if anything, than when it was first installed. We have found ways to cut down corrosion and to limit deterioration by electrolysis, ways to prevent rust. The new chromium-plating process which we are using on airplane parts, for example, makes this metal practically indestructible in so far as the influence of weather conditions on it is concerned. Rust-proof metals are being developed, we are finding ways to preserve wood, means of strengthening and preserving steel.

The point is, if there is enough thinking done along this line, there is no reason why we could not do the same with the human body. There is no law against it. The great problem is to get people in the mental attitude where they are willing to try to do it, willing to use the facts after we get them. There is a certain amount of mental inertia to be overcome in the promotion of any new thing. A few individuals may be quickly educated, but it takes time for society to move, to consent to the adoption of the new way.

Our hope is in the new generation. They accept new things more readily, because they have no false education, no preconceived ideas to reverse. They accepted the radio and the airplane as a part of their natural environment and could see no cause for wonder in the operation of either. So there is where education will begin—a practical education that will teach not only the "why" but the "how."

## Benefits of Prohibition

The gap between the people and their leaders is nowhere more discernible than in the matter of liquor. Some leaders are still for it; the people are now, as they have ever been, against it. The United States is dry not only legally but by moral conviction. You must find the people's sentiment where the people live. The American home is dry, and the American nation gets its tone from the home and not from the wet propagandist. In common decency the liquor generation should be allowed to die in silence. Its agonies should not be the constant topic of American journals.

Prohibition was intended to save the country and generations yet to come. There are a million boys growing up in the United States who have never seen a saloon, and who will never know the handicap of liquor, either in themselves or their relatives; and this excellent condition will go on spreading itself over the country when the wet press and the paid propaganda of booze are forgotten. There should be no mistake about it. The abolition of the commercialized liquor trade in this country is as final as the abolition of slavery. These are the two great reforms to which moral America committed itself from the beginning of its history.

Anything that interferes with our ability to think clearly, lead healthy, normal lives, and do our work well will ultimately be discarded, either as an economic handicap or from a desire for better personal health. Tobacco is a narcotic which is exacting a heavy toll from our present generation. No one smokes in the Ford industries. Tobacco is not a good thing for industry nor for the individual.

The coming of prohibition has put more of the workman's money into savings banks and into his wife's pocketbook. He has more leisure to spend with his family. The family life is healthier. Workmen go out of doors, go on picnics, have time to see their children and play with them. They have time to see more, do more—and, incidentally, they buy more. This stimulates business and *increases prosperity*, and in the general economic circle the money passes through industry again and back into the workman's pocket. It is a truism that what benefits one is bound to benefit all, and labor is coming to see the truth of this more every day.

Human demands are increasing every day and the needs for their gratification are increasing also. This is as it should be. Gradually, under the benign influence of American industry, wives are released from work, little children are no longer exploited; and, given more time, they both become free to go out and find new products, new merchants and manufacturers who are supplying them. Thus business grows. Thus we see the close relation which home life bears to industry. The prosperity of one is the prosperity of the other. In reality, all problems may be resolved into one great one. The parts are all interrelated one with another. The solution of one helps in the solution of another, and so on.

Machinery is accomplishing in the world what man has failed to do by preaching, propaganda, or the written word. The airplane and radio know no boundary. They pass over the dotted lines on the map without heed or hindrance. They are binding the world together in a way no other systems can. The motion picture with its universal language, the airplane with its speed, and the radio with its coming international programme—these will soon bring the whole world to a complete understanding. Thus may we vision a United States of the World. Ultimately, it will surely come!

## What Will the Future Know?

And yet with all our progress we know very little. We know nothing or comparatively nothing about the biggest thing or the smallest thing—little about the universe around us, and little about the atom. The microscope and the telescope are still limited instruments through which we see darkly. Yet I believe the time will come when man—in some one of his mental stages or planes of consciousness, if you wish to call it that—will know what is going on in the other planets, perhaps be able to visit them. When one looks back at the distance we have traveled mentally, in even the last fifty years, great things may be possible within the next century.

How do we think? What makes us think? Where do our thoughts come from? These are all interesting questions to me, interesting problems that I sometimes ponder. As with a properly tuned antenna, thoughts seem to come to one attuned to receive them. That seems to be the way we get ideas, but it takes a conscious effort on our part to be ready to receive them. Call this universal source of ideas anything you wish, the fact remains that the thoughts are all around us ready for acceptance. They come from outside of us, from a source that we may not know, but they are nevertheless available when we put ourselves into the right mental condition to receive them.

But the job of thinking is a real one—probably the hardest work there is to do. Yet I believe that all the world's secrets are open to thinkers, and that whenever a problem comes to us, it can always be solved—otherwise it would not present itself. I believe that we have always lived, moved, and had our being in this ocean of thought and that we shall always continue to live in it, even though our form and the form of the universe and things in it may change as we do.

# MY PHILOSOPHY OF
INDUSTRY

# MY PHILOSOPHY OF INDUSTRY

THERE is no denying the fact that life seems to be becoming more complicated. But is it, really? Isn't it rather that we are asked to make decisions more rapidly than before? With our new forms of transportation and communication the whole outlook of man is changed. It is greatly enlarged. He travels more, sees more, comes in contact with more people, does more things. But there is a question in my mind whether, with all this speeding up of our everyday activities, there is any more real thinking. Thinking is the hardest work there is, which is the probable reason why so few engage in it.

If it were possible first to teach people how to go to work to think and then to think, there would be hope for all sorts of things.

It is easy to have ideas. But whose are they and what are they worth? Merely having something on your mind is not thinking. Merely wondering is not thinking. Merely worrying is not thinking. Merely listening with all intentness to catch and remember something that some one is offering out of the essence of wisdom is not thinking. We all have intelligence, for intelligence is the ability to receive; but we have little thinking.

Thinking is creative or it is analytical. Intelligence comprehends the outlines of a thing. Thinking breaks it into its elements, analyzes it, and puts it together again. One feels, however, that—regardless of the fact that up to the present time everything has been about all that it could be under the circumstances—there is a sense in which from this moment forward a new era may emerge, if the necessary human components of the new era decide so. Perhaps the most one can hope for now is to drive home a conviction that as a people we have not done much thinking. If we think we have been thinking and then find out that we have not, the jolt of discovery may be of service to us.

The secrets of life are open to the thinker. Thinking is the work of digging to the foundation and has the aid of higher lights. Thinking calls for facts, and facts are found by digging. He who has gathered of this wealth is well equipped for life.

Of course, in the long run we never really create anything new. We merely discover something which has already existed. We know when we have reached Truth. We are on the right road toward Truth when the things that we are doing make men a little freer than they were. We may also know when we are on the right road by examining what our motives are. Of course, mistakes may be committed with right motives, but the general direction is right when the motive is right. These are the things of which we may be perfectly sure. These principles surround the very base of Life.

RIGHT THINGS IN THE WRONG WAY

In some instances we are doing right things in the wrong way. Because the method is wrong and the trouble begins presently to show the wrong results, people are quick to draw the conclusion that the whole thing is wrong. They want to wipe it all out. They want to overturn all the machinery of social and of political life. If that were the right thing to do, then it would be the right thing to do. We should never be fearful of the cost of the right thing.

Our discovery of Truth will be one of the great surprises of human experience. When the truth comes everywhere, it will be a great surprise to see how near we have been to it all the time without recognizing it, and to see how little are the changes to be made in our exterior mode of doing things. Our experience is a great preparation. It is a preparation to know the

Truth when we meet it. Of course, there are many ways of arriving at this goal. Men have been striving for it ever since civilization began. All right activity has been contributing to the ultimate result. Books, mechanics, commerce and science, the motor car, the radio, the airplane—all these have helped us on the way.

Our experiences are coming faster than ever before, both in our industrial world and in our domestic life. Many people see in these changes a world constantly growing worse. I do not believe this; I think we are headed in the right direction and that we should learn to interpret our new life rather than protest against it. We are entering a new era. Old landmarks have disappeared. Our new thinking and new doing are bringing us a new world, a new heaven, and a new earth, for which prophets have been looking from time immemorial. Much of it is here already. But I wonder if we see it.

I have no sympathy with those people who believe the world is growing worse. Of course, we all are making mistakes, but we learn by them. It is only when we correct these mistakes, reverse our tracks, and get back on the main road that we make progress. Automobiles that were made fifteen years ago no longer satisfy. We have all progressed, our needs have changed. We demand more, we see a wider horizon, a better type of civilization; and whether you believe that we are the originators of it or whether a wiser destiny has forced us to accept that which best promotes our welfare matters not.

That fact is here and we must recognize it and conform our manner of living to it.

The basic things are, of course, very old. Nothing useful ever passes away. If a light-headed group comes along and imagines they have found a new morality and if they draw to their books and plays and strange philosophies a following of other light-headed groups, some serious people are inclined to believe that the old morality has passed away. The good old type of goodness they say is gone. It is a rather foolish position to take and causes needless worry.

There is nothing new except a new appreciation, a new understanding, and this is the result of experience, and the result of experience can only be character. I believe that all we are here for is to get experience and form our character. Although our beginnings may be small, yet daily we are adding to our sum total of knowledge of reality—those eternalities of which real life is composed. I believe that our conscious individuality will never be lost. No matter what plane of thought we may inhabit we shall be in full consciousness of our birthright of thinking, and by each experience we shall improve our character.

Unfortunately, there exists in our day the pretense of a curious prejudice against any view of life that presupposes moral laws or values. The word "moral," like many other terms, has been narrowed in its meaning so that it has been made to serve in the very opposite sense. But when one regards the moral law as merely the law of right action or of truth it becomes quite different from "trying to be good." The universe is set in a certain direction, and when you go along with it, that is "goodness." If you don't, you are getting an admonitory kind of experience.

There is a vast difference between a man's being merely *statically* "good" and being *dynamically* good. In one state he is merely good negatively, and in the other he is good for something and puts that goodness into effect. He accomplishes something for mankind. We make no progress so long as we deny this. Our motive cannot be the attainment of some kind of goodness which is apart from life itself, but the attainment of inherent rightness, physically, mentally, spiritually, so that this complex instrument which we call society may efficiently function. The *right* way is the only *way*. The rightness of an attitude or method goes down through all its relations. Rightness in mechanics, rightness in morals are basically the same thing and cannot rest apart.

## Matter and Spirit

I make no difference between matter and spirit. They are different degrees of fineness of the same thing. The one is becoming the other, through ascent and descent, and both benefit by the process.

Will the poverty and the injustice and the need of the world force us to adopt this law of higher relations? If so, fortunate are we. When we speak of "morality in progress," we mean the maintenance by man of his control of the situation, instead of his being overwhelmed by the situation. We mean that he should mold progress to our highest concept of what is right between man and man and of what will work for the service of all, and not merely consent to be molded out of moral shape by the pressure of progress upon him.

Morality is merely doing the sound thing in the best way. It is a larger view and a longer view applied to life. The world is on the whole quite receptive to this implication of progress and we are all waiting for more manifestations of its workings, which are incidentally more numerous now than they have ever been in all the ages of mankind. Regardless of what we name it, this view is surely moving to practical recognition. There is one thing that we know about universal law:

it operates for us if we will, against us if it must—but it operates.

Furthermore, I believe that the application of this law is necessary for business success. Just as a clean factory, clean tools, accurate gauges, and precise methods of manufacture produce a smooth-working, efficient machine, so clear thinking, clean living, square dealing make of an industrial or domestic life a successful one, smooth-running and helpful to every one concerned. It has always been surprising to me that so few people realize this great fact. Many people are led astray by gaudily painted substitutes, imitations, when they could have the genuine for the same equivalent of time or money spent—in fact, many times for much less.

The whole industrial world is suffering

from many bad practices which we must refuse to use or tolerate. There must be a substitution of right methods, of right motives, the real ideas of service. I am no sentimentalist in this regard, it is just good business. There was a word once spoken which throws light on this: "Seek ye first the kingdom of God and His righteousness and all these things shall be added unto you." This is from the Sermon on the Mount. It sounds religious but it is just a plain statement of facts. It means just what it says—the reign, the rule, the law of the highest relations. Get that right way, work by that, and you have the world—a world without poverty, without injustice, without need.

As people wake up in their thinking—and we are even now arriving at this point in some respects—the benefits will be universally ours. Such facts are spreading throughout the whole civilized world. Even foreign lands are feeling the benefit of American progress, our American right thinking. Both Russia's and China's problems are fundamentally industrial and will be solved by the application of these right methods of thinking, practically applied.

## No Machine Age

Another thing, it is a mistake to think that we are living in a *machine age*. That's one of those bugaboos which people who do not understand the changing fundamentals of our civilization have set up. They prophesy all sorts of things because we have been freeing men for centuries and making it possible for them to widen their lives. We are *not* living in a machine age, *we are living in the power age.* This power age of ours has great possibilities, depending upon how we use it. Of course it can be abused. But it can also be used greatly to benefit mankind.

Here is where what we call the moral law comes in. Power must be properly used or it will destroy us. But I, for one, do not believe that we are headed in this direction. I believe that, fundamentally, every man has sensed his freedom and is eagerly making way for the new era, which is fast appearing. I think we are due for a big change in educational methods. That is one of the reasons why we are, at present, trying out our trade school form of teaching.

Give men or women the ability to think for themselves and they will soon acquire the facts necessary for the solution of their problems. The ability to recognize truth when you see it and the ability to think a thing through to its logical conclusion—these are important. These will help a man or woman contribute his or her share to the social welfare and progress of the world.

Abraham Lincoln and Benjamin Franklin both thought in fundamentals. They would be just as much at home in our civilization of to-day—just as valuable contributing members of our society—as they were in the age in which they lived. The Truth they knew still persists. The Truth we discover, know, and use, sets our value in the world.

In the deep, unwritten wisdom of life, there are many things to be learned that cannot be taught. We never know them by hearing them spoken, but we grow into them by experience and recognize them through understanding. Understanding is a great experience in itself, but it does not come through instruction. Nothing ripens that is not first planted, and the very desire, the dream, the ambitions of youth are by way of a planting which will come to fruition some time after these desires are abandoned and forgotten. For the sown seed goes on growing whether we remember it or not. The wisdom of life is to keep on planting.

It seems to be the tendency of our coming generation to want things in tabloid form. Our youth want to get their education quickly. They want to find short cuts to knowledge. In some ways this is a desirable tendency. We are making use of it in our trade schools by teaching our boys many things by motion pictures. For example, we teach them how to use a micrometer, how to use gauges. Many of the processes which are hard to describe in words can be made plain in a few moments by good pictures. Pictures speak the universal language. But, on the other hand, observation means little without reflection. In the old methods we observed many things pretty much as they really were. In the present-day radio and movie we observe them as some one desires them to appear.

Such a process is likely to stunt our reflective power. On the other hand, the new methods are stimulants. However, these new mediums of education will gradually find their place and the outworn methods will slip out. This will, of course, happen in individual cases much faster than it will in society generally. As is always the case, individuals can make more rapid progress than society can. One portion of the country or the world may see a thing and use it for months or even years before the rest of the world is willing to adopt it.

To my mind there is little difference between an international problem and a local one. The only difference is that people generally think in local terms instead of thinking in universal conceptions. As I have told many young men who have come to me for advice on how to succeed, it is just as easy to think big as it is to think in small and limited ways. It is just as easy to plow a thousand acres with a tractor as it used to be to plow a ten-acre lot with a horse. And it takes no more time.

## Politics Don't Matter

Political boundaries and political opinions don't really make much difference. It is the economic condition which really forces change and compels progress.

I have been asked several times whether I believe that the large cities will continue to grow and drain the country of its small town population, or whether the reverse will be true. Well, I think we shall continue to have large cities and small towns. Each has its advantage, each has its reason for being. There are disadvantages in both, but the good in each will survive. The father and mother of to-day, who are not content with the conditions under which they are living, will not be willing to have their children grow up in the same environment. They will try to change it and thus will come about many movements which will be good for both the city and the country.

Our new forms of transportation are making it easy for people to get out to see other localities, to become familiar with the kind of country in which they wish to settle. Such an interchange of social contacts, such a broadening of all people's geographical horizons will ultimately bring about a redistribution in which each person will naturally gravitate to that part of the country in which he is best satisfied to live. The automobile has done for this country what the airplane and radio may do for the world. A wider circulation of right ideas always breaks down prejudices and helps secure universal understanding.

This, then, suggests a solution of the problem of world peace. A peaceful nation is one that has the means to make war and refrains. Until the means are present, disposition toward their misuse cannot be fully known. In the present world the believers in peace confront the advocates of war and, fortunately, the former are better armed. Their power for peace seems to be in proportion to their power to enforce it.

It sometimes seems that the course of history has been an effort to produce the invincible warrior and through him to dominate the world for peace. The nation must be capable of making war and refrain before its natural peaceableness can be known. Some nations, very great ones, are to-day physically unable to make war. Maybe they will continue peaceable even when they become capable of this dread ability, but we also know that there are nations able to make war who believe in peace. What the peace-loving forces of the world are facing is the war-loving forces. If that fact could be realized much waste motion would be saved.

It is interesting to study international methods of education. The educational processes differ according to the goal in view. Many of the old civilizations educate their upper classes for a condition of economic freedom and vegetative leisure,

## MY PHILOSOPHY OF INDUSTRY

while their lower classes are held in industrial slavery. In fact, it is by the use of leisure that we may judge the characteristics of a people. There was a time when leisure was regarded as lost time. Particularly in industry, the creation of leisure time was supposed to be impractical and wasteful. It was said that working men had not been trained how to make the most of it and that a reduction of daily working hours would result in greater poverty and dissipation.

We, in America, have changed our thoughts in this regard very much during the last few years. We have come to see that leisure is not waste time, that even from a cold business point of view it pays dividends in greater profits, better health, and a better product. Furthermore, it has been discovered that the workingman very soon finds a desirable and healthy way to use his leisure time to his own personal advancement and for the greater happiness of his family. The second generation is never at a mental loss to improve their time. It has been our experience that even those who come from countries where long, hard working hours were the rule are soon found using their leisure hours in a useful manner.

Man needs leisure to think, and the world needs thinkers. One of the hardest things in the industrial world to-day is to find enough men who are capable of thinking a problem through, executives who can do the whole job without further supervision or additional prompting. Americans of every class have more spare time

## MY PHILOSOPHY OF INDUSTRY

than the people of any other nation in the world. But leisure is by no means secure so long as it is regarded as a privilege forced by the demands of the class. It is not secure so long as industry regards it as lost time. There is a law which definitely relates leisure to economic well-being. We are learning to use that law to the betterment of our business, the improvement of our people, and the increased welfare of our country.

# SUCCESS

## SUCCESS

STUDENTS of world progress recognize that there is a time for everything. Like the opening of a flower or the budding of a tree, certain events cannot be forced ahead of their time; nor, conversely, can they be disregarded after the time for their appearance has come. Therefore it behooves the man—especially the young man—who wishes to have his part in the progress of this world, to watch the signs of the times and be ready at the proper moment to take his place in the procession of human events.

Not only in industry, but in all lines of work is this so. In the scheme of progress each unit has its logical place, which no other can fill. As a case in point, the automobile and the airplane could not be successfully developed until the internal combustion engine had been invented. Earlier engines, such as steam engines, were too heavy; they weighed too much per horsepower to be practical for use in these two new vehicles of transportation. But with the coming of the internal combustion engine it was possible to concentrate in a small place and a small weight an enormous amount of power. Thus it enabled us to develop the automobile, and, later on, the airplane. One invention makes way for another; one discovery lights up the path ahead so that he who runs may read—and lead.

Similarly, the development of industry

was long delayed because one link in the chain of progress was missing. When that had been forged, industry shot ahead to its present high rate of production. I refer to the matter of long-distance power transmission. Back in the days when machinery had to be run by steam or water power, cables and belts were the only means of power transmission. This meant that factories had to be located in the immediate neighborhood of the plant, or on the bank of the stream from which power was derived. The natural tendency was for industry to group itself around large sources of power. Thus centralization was brought about, and on its heels followed quantity production. The mere idea of quantity production was a great step forward, but its concentration was hampered by the very condition that had given rise to it. So long as centralization was necessary, so long as manufacturing could be carried on only by the limited number of factories that could crowd around the various sources of power, quantity production on the present scale was impossible.

### THE MISSING LINK IN THE CHAIN OF PROGRESS

Then within our knowledge—within our century—electricity was discovered. Electricity possessed this great advantage over all other kinds of power previously produced: it could be instantaneously transmitted over great distances by wire. Power could be generated in one spot and sent out to any number of factories all over the country. The necessity for centralization had been eliminated, and manufacturing went ahead on a larger scale than ever.

Light, heat, and power—think what has been accomplished by this one idea put into action! And the power age has barely begun. In our own shops we are constantly improving our method of manufacture, with an eye to efficiency, economy, and the safety and comfort of our employees. Belt transmission has been entirely supplanted by electrically driven machines, which frees us from the danger and annoyance of wheels and belts whirling overhead. Our furnaces, most of which are electrically heated, are so constructed and insulated that the men work in front of them without discomfort. There is no smoke or gas except in a few processes, and, in these, electric ventilators carry off all disagreeable odors and unhealthful fumes.

The increase in the scale of production does not mean that craftsmanship has gone. From the earliest times machines of some sort have been in use. It took craftsmen to make and use machines then, and it takes craftsmen now. The hand and the brain and the eye have functioned together ever since man came upon the earth. The hand-made age is still with us, but it has been refined and advanced until it stands on a higher plane than when men used wooden plows and primitive potters' wheels. We value the things of the past because of their association; they were steps toward those of the present. But as needs have grown, means of production have been increased and improved.

# SUCCESS

It has been asserted that machine production kills the creative ability of the craftsman. This is not true. The machine demands that man be its master; it compels mastery more than the old methods did. The number of skilled craftsmen in proportion to the working population has greatly increased under the conditions brought about by the machine. They get better wages and more leisure in which to exercise their creative faculties.

There are two ways of making money—one at the expense of others, the other by service to others. The first method does not "make" money, does not create anything; it only "gets" money—and does not always succeed in that. In the last analysis, the so-called gainer loses. The second way pays twice—to maker and user, to seller and buyer. It receives by creating, and receives only a just share, because no one is entitled to all. Nature and humanity supply too many necessary partners for that. True riches make wealthier the country as a whole.

Most people will spend more time and energy in going around problems than in trying to solve them. A problem is a challenge to your intelligence. Problems are only problems until they are solved, and the solution confers a reward upon the solver. Instead of avoiding problems we should welcome them and through right thinking make them pay us profits. The discerning youth will spend his time learning *direct methods,* learning how to make his brain and hand work in harmony with each other so that the problem in hand may be solved in the simplest, most direct way that he knows.

### The Dead Limbs of Life

We can get rid of a tremendous number of the bothersome things of life if we put our minds to it. The number of needless tasks that are performed daily by thousands of people is amazing. It is the work of men with vision to trim out some of these dead limbs of life. Some of our industrial leaders have already done a good job in their own front yards, but the commons of life need attention too. Trimming out dead wood hurts no one. After all is said and done, our one great problem is the problem of life itself, of which industry is one of the tributary activities.

It is easier to denounce a wrong than to

tackle the job of curing it. We cannot evade our job by blaming the past. The past took care of itself, and it depends on us to take care of the present. Many things that were thought in the past to be right we have found to be wrong. But—and remember this—none of the things believed to be thoroughly wrong have we found to be right. Even wrong things have to pass through a period of being thought right before they can be known as wrong. When we find out their nature, our responsibility begins. It is this generation's duty to the next to start at once to make room for the right thing.

Our fathers thought that life was hard, but we are beginning to see how preventable some of its hardships are. We have come to believe that there is no necessity for economic distress in a world so richly furnished with resources. Men are searching with sharp eyes for the defects in our system which prevents a man from working when he wants to work and his responsibilities require it. Economic stoppage is not natural. This defect is not in the created order of things; it is in the human order. Our selfishness, our lack of wisdom have created it. If we have established a money system which can be manipulated to the hurt of multitudes, it is as certain as fate that the system is doomed. The very discovery of insufficiency is its death warrant.

### Something Rotten in Economics

Some people think that everything will be rectified when war is abolished. Well, let nothing interfere with the abolition of war. But sound thinking insists that war will not be abolished until its roots are cut; and one of its main roots is a false money system and the high priests thereof. But more of that later. What causes war is not patriotism, not that human beings are willing to die in defense of their dearest ones. It is the false doctrine, fostered by the few, that war spells gain. It is this that makes war, and there are not enough pacifists who see it and attack it. The fact that pacifists are left in peace is proof they are not attacking the real causes of war. If pacifists spoke the truth, they would not be petted as they are to-day; theirs would be the hard lot of the martyrs of Truth.

We often speak of the ignorance of the past; but our distant forefathers were no more ignorant than we. They were grinding the grist of experience through the mills of the mind, and were discovering what was good and what was bad for them. That is all we are doing. What will be known in the future as the ignorance of this present generation is just the residue of discoveries which we shall not have time to make. Our responsibility is not to create a perfect world, but to establish our discoveries of what is right by weeding out what we have newly discovered to be wrong, leaving to the future its task of the same nature.

One of the principal duties that devolve during periods of change is the duty of *conscious allegiance*. To-day, conscious allegiance costs something. At the very first it means division between those who are loyal to moral convictions and those who are not. The majority of the people are naturally straddlers. They are not in the world to pioneer but to be as happy as possible. If pioneering in a cause brings discomfort, they would rather not be among the pioneers. They would rather stand on the side lines and, in the combat between truth and error, wait and see which proves the stronger. Though they may have a lazy faith that truth at last will win, they do not wish to lend a premature support. Yet majorities are essential, not to the truth, but to the acknowledgment of the truth. There are some opposites in the world that should never be reconciled. There are some programs that should never be harmonized. What frightens some people is that they want to be happy, to live and let live without being bothered. They would like to enjoy the world as it is, and if there are those who would improve the world, let them do so—but not in a way that interferes with their present happiness.

The most important work that faces the young generation to-day is making the world a better place to live in. There are thousands of great tasks waiting to be accomplished. There are innumerable opportunities in the three great arts—agriculture, industry, and transportation. The youth who can solve the money question will do more for the world than all the professional soldiers of history.

# MY PHILOSOPHY OF INDUSTRY

## The Three Principal Arts

I have often said that mankind passes from the old to the new on a human bridge formed by those who labor in the three principal arts—agriculture, manufacture, transportation. We are a bridge generation. The complaints that we hear concerning the slowness of the world's change from worse to better come mostly from people who would rather be the crossing throng than help support the bridge upon which humanity passes. Fortunately for all of us, ours is not the choice.

There is a group of people who believe that the millennium will be brought about by a new system of distribution. They do not realize the fundamental truth that all things of value have always been distributed. The problem is to *use* them. It takes thinking, and there is no substitute for that. All the treasure chests of industry may be unlocked by this key. Look at our natural resources, our undeveloped water power, our unused forces of nature. Often a single right idea put into action is enough to make them mankind's slaves.

The truth of things escapes us, mostly because truth is so simple. Truth is a seed within itself; its nature is to reveal itself first to one or two, then ultimately to all. At a pace dependent upon our receptivity and in a manner measured by our mentality, we must do the work that destiny has given us if we would pass on to the next generation its rightful heritage. Don't be afraid of the changing order. It may look like chaos, but when the passing débris of the old has been cleared away, there will be found a thousand new opportunities teeming with promise and power.

## Talkers and Doers

Youth has one great element in its favor—it can live in the future. The world of to-morrow belongs to the young man of to-day; he can begin shaping the world now. No age has ever presented the tremendous opportunities of the present, but along with these opportunities are proportionate responsibilities. With the changing wheel of ambition, boys no longer regard the talkative professions as more important than the manual. They realize that there are gigantic tasks to be done and that these will be accomplished by doers rather than talkers. The man who does things is vastly more important to the world than the clerk who merely makes the record of others' achievements.

Youths have a tremendous advantage over their elders in possessing the power of vision without the drawback of retrospect. They bring fresh eyes and fresh minds to old tasks. They are not tied down by the traditions of the past; they are not slaves to the failures of others. Their concern is not so much with what could have been done in the past as with what can be done in the future. What they make of it will depend on what they make of themselves and the opportunities or tasks which are now before them.

Of course, education has its limits. Education and ability to do things are not interchangeable terms. You cannot educate brains into a man's head, but you can help him to make the most of the brains he has. A man who cannot think is not an educated man, no matter how many college degrees he may have acquired. One who can think things out usually can do them. An education which consists of signposts indicating the failures and fallacies of the past is doubtless useful. Many men are at work to-day on theories fundamentally wrong, ignorant that other men have followed that road and have had to come back. So schools are useful if they show the blind alleys of human endeavor. Then they must help to put men in possession of their own powers. But they cannot do this without the earnest desire of their students to be so helped. Inventors, by the way, are not made by education; but if they have enough education to spare them the mistakes of the past, it saves their time.

Most of us are doing two things—that by which the body is kept alive, and that by which the higher part of our nature lives. We go to the job to pay expenses and then we indulge ourselves in what we like to do and maybe were meant to do. The whole secret of a successful life is to find out what it is one's destiny to do, and then do it. Some day there may come to one the duty to do a disagreeable task, to take up a cause which will yield no reward—a cause which will at first surround one with misunderstanding and abuse, and which will make one look like a fool before men. One naturally shrinks from it. But when a man is sure of what he has to do, he should go ahead full speed. To be right means mainly to be in tune with destiny and willing to obey. It does not necessarily mean to be agreeable, nor to be agreed with, nor to be popular; it does mean to be useful in the purpose which destiny is trying to achieve in us and through us. If a man is right, he need not fear to stand alone; he is not alone. Every right idea that is put forth has many silent adherents.

There is a great deal of nonsense spoken about the "lonely heights"—they may seem to be lonely, but they are only silent. The loneliness comes when a man settles within himself whether he is to be a mere form following a conventional routine or whether he is to listen and obey the voice of a changeable life. It is lonely while he

# SUCCESS

is deciding. If he decides to do what duty bids him, then he is no longer lonely. He comes at once into the fellowship of other people who are thinking as he is, but who have been waiting for a leader to declare them and their principles.

# WHY I BELIEVE IN PROGRESS

## WHY I BELIEVE IN PROGRESS

A SATISFACTORY life is one that fulfills to the highest measure one's capacity for achievement, and then widens and deepens and develops that measure so that the man becomes bigger and better than his success. We can have only the experiences we are able to receive and make use of, the rest slip by us. The two great hindrances to success are fear and pride. It is easy to tell a man to get rid of fear, and another thing to tell him how. A careful analysis of his fears and a study of their causes will many times reveal a solution and show him how really futile they are.

Much of the opposition to industrial reorganization comes from pride. If you go into a shop and try to put it on a basis of successful operation, you will find that in nine cases out of ten the things you have to change are the very things in which some one takes an inordinate pride. The instances where pride has proved a hindrance in business are so numerous that one could quote them without end. A little observation will show that a man given to pride is usually proud of the wrong thing.

Now in business, the job is the thing— when men are job-centered, they are less self-centered and there is therefore less soil for the interference of personal likes and dislikes, personal pride and personal prejudices. If there is any pride, it is centered in the job; if there is any prejudice, it is with reference to the job. Any method is willingly revised or abandoned; any cherished theory is immediately scrapped; any personal element is completely sunk in the great general importance of the job. If the job isn't big enough to command this sort of allegiance in a man, he should make it big enough; and if he can't do that, he should find one that is big enough.

The wrong kind of pride does not contribute anything. It deceives the man who harbors it and hinders every one within the radius of its malign influence. It has wrecked careers that might have been useful. When a man falls in love with *his* way, *his* method, *his* system, and exalts them to the place of first importance; when he resents competent criticism and change designed to focus his attention and efforts on a central job, he is on the down grade. So my advice to young men is to be ready to revise any system, scrap any methods, abandon any theory if the success of the job requires it. The more readily we scrap these things, the less danger is there to our fundamental principles—which ought never to be scrapped, on any pretense whatever.

There are many things more valuable than money—time, energy, and material are worth more than money, because they cannot be purchased by money. It is a rather strange arrangement of nature that only the most precious values can be wasted. You can waste time, you can waste labor, and you can waste material, that is about all—you cannot waste money. You can misuse money but you cannot waste it, it is still somewhere. You can waste your own opportunity or may use it for your benefit. To use what you have is much better than to save what you have. Economy is no cure for waste, use is the word.

Some would substitute the word "economy" for "use." This is wrong. The word economy represents a half-idea born of fear. Everything is given to us to use. There is no evil from which we suffer that did not come to us through misuse. There is no function which human beings can fulfill that is not good, but we have all about us a spectacle of whole nations having to make laws against things, not bad fundamentally, but bad in the way they are used. The worst possible sin we can commit against the things of our common life is to misuse them. There are two kinds of waste—that of the prodigal who misuses his substance and that of the sluggard who allows his substance to rot through non-use; both are creators of waste. The strict economizer is in danger of being classed with the sluggard. The remedy in both instances is *use*.

## THE VALUE OF MISTAKES

Mistakes, whether they occur in the social realm or in the building of a new machine, are often the result of active research. The mind knows the end which it wishes to reach, it sees an opening, enters it, and explores far enough to discover that the opening does not lead where the mind wishes to go. Another opening is explored in a like manner and withdrawn from, so that experience is gained at every step. This is not waste, it is not evil, it is not blameworthy; it is a part of the material of knowledge. This negative knowledge may be in the back of your mind unused, but it is a part of knowledge just the same. Within our range of knowledge and necessity we have made certain things work and we have found certain principles. On the other hand we know that certain things will not work. This positive and negative knowledge is all useful. There should be no worrying over mistakes, because mistakes are part of the material of experience. It is a mistake, however, to scrap a thing because it is defective without first ascertaining what caused it to fail and whether the defect can be remedied. More knowledge is thus gained. We need analysis more than faultfinding, for then we face conditions. From analysis we can go on to proper criticism, and from proper analysis and criticism should emerge a better weighing of values, a better way of doing the job—in other words, real progress.

It is amazing to observe how large a percentage of our intelligent people desire to remain in the region of faultfinding simply because it calls for too strenuous an effort of the mind to rise into the region of analysis. The analyst takes the situation apart and lays the facts bare. Then comes the power of criticism, which means the weighing of values, the rating of all facts according to universal standards. Faultfinding is emotional, analysis is intellectual, criticism is moral. It is only when these flower into creativeness that the full value of the achievement becomes evident, but therein lies the real value of an education—to get something worth while done, something that will benefit all mankind and put civilization in debt to the doer. That, to my mind, is success—and something worth striving for.

What portion of progress is due to effort and what portion to the pressure of destiny no one can say. Men are pushed ahead oftener than they go ahead of their own will—that is, mankind in the mass. This pressure may sometimes be due to the appearance of a new personality with a new idea, or it may be due to a combination of circumstances too big for any person to cause or control. As an illustration, a new invention may force society to reorganize certain of its activities, a new idea may force political changes, a new form of power distribution may completely overturn industrial practice. All of us have seen these things happen in our own generation. At these times of reversal it takes clear vision to steer a straight path. Men with old ideas cling to old ways of doing things, frequently attempting to solve the new problems by old methods. But new men soon rise to take their place—men who have read the signs of the times aright and who are flexible enough and wise enough to interpret rather than protest the changing order.

The instinct of the people is to look for prophets, and, of course, there are plenty of people who are willing to pose in this capacity. The false prophet is usually an honest gentleman whose main error is in posing as a prophet. One fundamental difference between him and the true prophet is in the matter of popularity. The false prophet cannot live without it, the other must. One who seeks popularity must obey the laws of popularity, but the true prophet is mastered by other considerations. He is charged with something he must deliver. He may be keenly sensitive to the offense and pain which truth so often inflicts; but he has no choice. To win acceptance is not his problem. His whole responsibility rests with utterance. Utterance is so important to truth that he cannot rest until he speaks. He may not talk much about his destiny, but he is conscious of its burden, of the inescapable urge which forces him to the thing that he was born to do. He may shrink from its consequences, but he cannot shrink from the duty. He knows that utterance is the sharp flying wedge of truth which must infallibly cleave its way through all opposition to a general acceptance. He may not see this at once. He may only see through all his career the gathering forces that oppose his truth; but he knows that this very gathering of opposition is providential, for it is being gathered and headed up so that it may be destroyed together.

Reading the signs of the times is a method of information open to every one. The two essentials of wisdom are a knowledge of fundamentals and an awareness of their development. To know *what is growing* and in *what direction* it is growing comprises the highest providential wisdom—it is the ability to read the signs of the times, not of the times that are, but the times that are to be.

People who try to understand only the immediate times are somewhat behind the times. Those who know the times at all began to understand them before they existed. Signs of the times, then, are the signs of the times to come. The signs of the times that now are were given long ago. By the time they emerge into actuality they are no longer signs, they are the times themselves. It is one thing to see a thing, another thing to see through a thing. There is very little of life on the surface. We see to-day as the product of distant yesterdays; yet hidden in to-day is a root of distant to-morrows, and it is the man who knows the coming to-morrows who really sees most of life. To read the signs of the times one must do a kind of original work—read what few are reading, or, I might say, read what isn't yet printed, reach original conclusions, deal with fundamental values which lie beneath and behind all other values. One leads the way for himself instead of following others, one looks to principles, to a deep foundation upon which rest the changes that afterward occur. The signs of the times demand our learning a new language, observing fundamental things, doing original thinking, getting at naked facts, and being sure that they *are* facts, not simply theories. Life is a river which constantly changes its course, and the way of understanding is to follow this river—not the dried up and deserted river bed.

## THE EXTRAVAGANCE OF GOVERNMENT FINANCING

Of what use is all this? Well, let's apply it to a specific economic problem. Take the money question for example. Suppose we in the United States find ourselves with some public improvement work to do, the development of some of our natural resources. The usual way the government sets about doing this sort of thing is to issue bonds—say for thirty years—and to sell them to the highest bidder. Then they go ahead and hire workmen to do the job, pay them with the money received from the proceeds of the sale of bonds, and then at the end of thirty years pay back the bondholders together with interest. What happens in the process? In the first place, what makes the bonds valuable? Why are people willing to buy them? Well, because the United States Government stands behind them; in other words, the government is putting up security for its own loans, and the security which it puts up is nothing more nor less than the energy of wealth in its most productive form, *i.e.*, natural resources. It is the best security in the world, security that survives the wreck of banks and treasuries.

So then, if we start with a security which is unquestioned and which the people are willing to accept as collateral for the bonds issued, why should we go through the complicated and unnecessary process of paying 120 per cent interest out of our own pocket to somebody else for the privilege of getting $30,000,000

## WHY I BELIEVE IN PROGRESS

which, in reality, we already own? Take a piece of paper and a pencil and figure it out for yourself. Suppose we borrow $30,000,000 and pay 120 per cent interest, we literally have to pay $66,000,000 for the use of the $30,000,000. That is, we pay $30,000,000 for the public improvement and $36,000,000 for the loan. And it was the government's own money to begin with! It seems like a very childish and unbusinesslike method.

Now here is a way I see by which our government can get great work completed on a less complicated plan. It is a sound way, but there is one thing hard about it; it is so simple and easy that maybe some people can't see it. Suppose, for example, we desire to relieve unemployment by carrying on some necessary public improvement, and to do this the government needs $30,000,000. That's a million and half twenty dollar bills or three million ten dollar bills. The government can issue these against the value of the thing in prospect and with them pay every expense connected with the work, then put the plant in operation and out of its earnings retire the entire $30,000,000 worth of currency which has been issued. Economists no longer question that method of doing things. Indeed, it looks as if financial engineering will come round to something very like it. We shall see great improvement when we apply engineering methods to finance.

Gold and money are two entirely different things. Gold is a metal of value to the arts, but of no real intrinsic value as money until the government stamps it with its authoritative mark—that is, coins it as money. Actual money is ability to buy, a measure of credit, a sort of scales or simple method of bookkeeping between the buyer and seller used as a substitute for the actual transference of commodities one to another. We can use anything for a medium of exchange that is durable and controllable and scarce enough. Gold happens to be fairly scarce. It is durable and controllable. But it has disadvantages, too. It becomes dearer and cheaper—it fluctuates like everything else. Furthermore, it can be privately manipulated, and therein lies the danger. We should have a currency system which cannot be made the catspaw of manipulators. As long as money is in circulation and being used for productive purposes, it is performing its function; but when it is cornered or kept out of circulation—ignorantly or for malicious purposes—then the "money question" becomes serious.

Of course, I do not advocate the upsetting of the money system. We don't need to abolish anything. We do not even need to abolish the gold standard. We need only to observe the principle of use to which I have referred. We need the principles of social engineering. The benefit should always be public—that is, general. Service always pays better than selfishness, although sometimes it takes centuries for the people to see this. The more alert financial men of this country are thinking of these matters on broader lines than ever before, and that is very heartening, for, after all, financial problems will have to be handled by financial minds. The rank and file of our people are able to see how things ought to be, but the specialists will have to create the methods by which the "ought-to-be" will actually come into practice.

## Business Men as Social Leaders

Business men do not think of themselves as leaders in social movements, but they are. Not a single system of business exists —good or bad—but has been taught to the people by business men. They have more influence on society than politicians, schoolmasters, or clergymen, because their contact is constant and their influence unavoidable. Every bad habit of unthrift and debt is taught the people by their business guides. Their leadership should turn around and head in the opposite direction. Business men should be readers of the signs of the time to warn the people to wise action and safe building on sound foundations. To be a business man is to assume the responsibility of economic leadership. No wrong economic practice, no disastrous system of doing business could possibly get a foothold except through the local business man.

There is no dangerous business practice in existence to-day that was not deliberately taught to the people, forced upon the people, by men who had no thought of the general social benefit. Teaching and leading the people to invest wisely, to begin getting things that make their lives more productive of real values is one thing;

teaching them to forget their natural abhorrence of debt, leading them to forego their independence by working for a small army of installment collectors is quite another thing. If the careful, constructive attitude of the average family toward its economic responsibilities has been lowered, it is the result of systematic false education by a certain type of business system.

Now, when these things begin to appear and to flourish, the wise man sees a sign of coming danger and prepares for it. Systems wrongly based cannot succeed; they must fail and the colossal extent of everything we do in America brings the failure earlier and makes it harder than it would otherwise be. The self-limited business can weather any gale, but vast enterprises built on a gamble of other people's extravagance collapse at once. People who can see the signs of the times begin their own reformation. Those who are in places of leadership lend their good counsel. If the signs are observed soon enough, the situation is changed and we have gained some experience which will prevent a repetition of the mistake.

At present there is far less poverty in this country than ever before. Our material life is on a much higher level than it has ever been. But comparing the present with what it ought to be and what it could be, we cannot fail to see that much is yet to be done. Far more people, however, can be persuaded to relieve poverty than to devote their energies to removing it. Charity is no substitute for reform. Poverty is not cured by charity, it is only relieved. To cure it the cause of the trouble must be located and then removed. Nothing does more to abolish poverty than work. Every man who works is helping to drive poverty away.

It is not the men who are doing the talking who are solving our problems, but the men who are at work. Nobody can think straight who does not work, for idleness warps the mind. It is a wonder that we do not hear more about that fact, that the practiced hand gives balance to the brain. Thinking which does not connect with constructive action becomes a disease. The man who has it sees crooked; his views are lopsided. No man can think out our great problems for us. We believe in democracy because we believe that the collective mind is better than the single mind. With the people thinking together and planning together and acting together the greatest advances are possible.

Every age teems with theories requiring only to stand a while before their falsity will be revealed. We don't have to test every theory that is offered. Let it stand. If it is right, it will endure; if it is wrong, the public mind simply outgrows it. No one can imagine how much worse off we should be if we followed every theory and every leader that promised us the Golden Age. So if our progress seems slow, it is only because of the people's carefulness not to make a misstep. But there is progress being made at all times, now in this direction and now in that. Such progress is a social creation. It is the people moving up, and that is the only kind of progress there is.

## WHY I BELIEVE IN PROGRESS

If we have not yet gone forward rapidly, there is a very great fact to be set against that fact: the human race has not had to retrace many steps because of false moves.

**THE END**

CPSIA information can be obtained
at www.ICGtesting.com
Printed in the USA
LVOW04s0250230617
539109LV00026B/1042/P